My Room is a Black Hole

My Room is a Black Hole

Grateful the Dinosaur Press

My Room is a Black Hole

Published by: Grateful the Dinosaur Press

Grateful for Science Series # 1

Copyright © 2024 by Jose Guzman

ISBN 978-1-0691533-0-2

For my mom

My mom says the pile of clothes on my bedroom floor is so big that nothing, not even light, can escape from it.

So big and with so many clothes exploded and spiraling across my bedroom floor, the pile of clothes, the matter attracts even more,

It gets bigger... the pile of clothes on my bedroom floor grows more and more across space and time.

My gym shorts and even my fancy dress pants thrown so closely and densely one on top of the other. The matter and mass around them cause more clothes and shoes to join the pile.

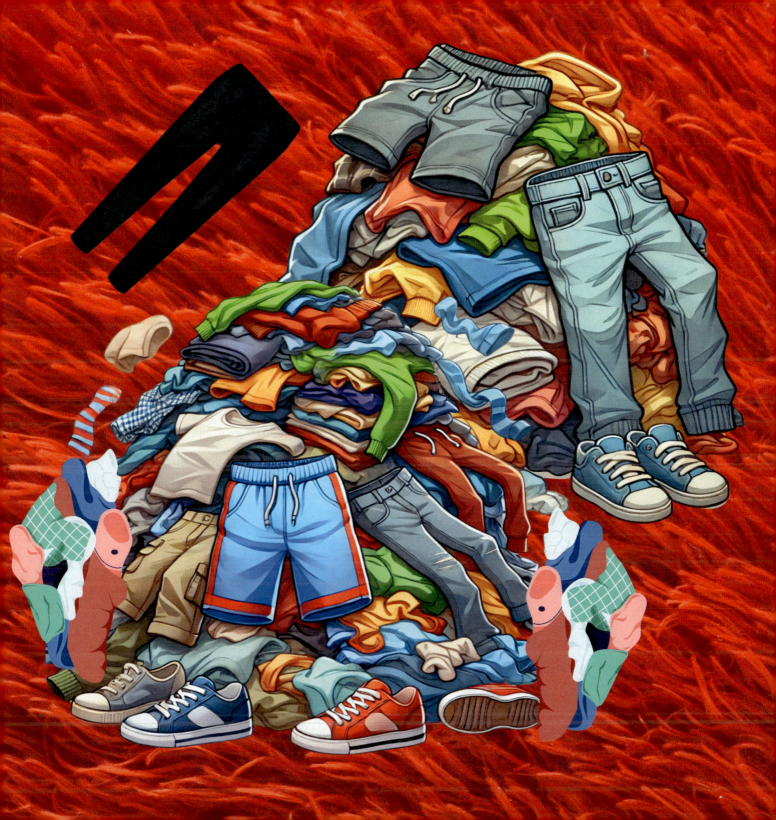

Like my T-shirts and hoodies,
none of my clothes are safe from
falling.

Falling...

Falling... into and becoming a part of the supermassive black hole pile of clothes.

My room is a black hole. Piles and piles of dirty clothes all packed densely and close on my bedroom floor.

If my favorite T-shirt, for instance, my Dad's cool vintage band tee from the 90s, got too close to the pile, it would fall, past the point of no return, into the event horizon.

The event horizon is the beginning and the end of my Dad's cool vintage T-shirt from the 90s... it has passed the boundary, disappeared, stretched out, and joined the matter of dirty clothes. I cannot see it anymore, it has become the black hole.

If my socks fell inside the event horizon, they would immediately stretch out and spaghettify.

All matter, like my socks, are squeezed horizontally and stretched vertically looking like strands of spaghetti. My giant pile of dirty, smelly spaghetti socks.

At the center of the pile of clothes on my bedroom floor is the singularity, an area where my shoes, gym shorts, and even my fancy dress pants, hoodies, and T-shirts, including my Dad's, and even my socks sit packed together so densely and tightly. I can't tell them apart anymore, there is only the black hole.

I'm scared I might become a part of it too. Under the socks, shirts, hoodies, shoes, fancy dress pants, and shorts... I would fall into the black hole and be lost forever in the darkness of space and at the end of time.

But suddenly, my Mom and Dad come into my bedroom and say, it's time to clean up your bedroom floor, then it's time for dinner, and then it's almost the end of the day.

So, I grab three piles of clothes under my arms, and my supermassive black hole shrinks and becomes like it's stellar, named just like the stars in the falling night sky.

And with any luck, I too will soon fall,
but not like the sky or into a black hole,
but asleep on the couch after dinner
and free of any more laundry today.

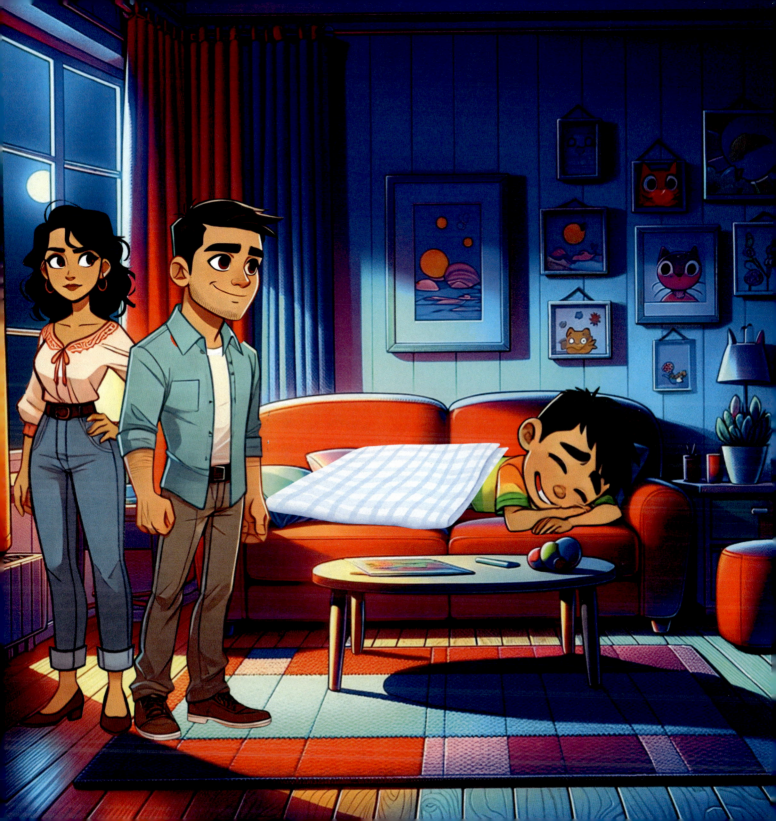

The black hole pile of clothes on my bedroom floor remains and who knows, it might even grow.

My Room is a Black Hole

Grateful the Dinosaur Press

Manufactured by Amazon.ca
Bolton, ON